Countertop In...

FAVORITE RECIPES FROM
GRANDMA'S KITCHEN

120 TASTY RECIPES

BARBOUR

INSPIRATION
at your fingertips!

Looking for a simple way to bring new life to your kitchen? This book is for you. Within these pages, you'll find dozens of tasty recipes that are just like Grandma used to make and are a delight to share with family and friends.

Finding a recipe is as easy as flipping through the book. Along the edge of each page, you'll see a color that corresponds to one of five categories:

Main Dishes & Casseroles . . . **(p. 5)**

Soups, Salads & Vegetables . .**(p. 33)**

Cakes, Cookies & Sweets . . .**(p. 61)**

Appetizers & Beverages . . . .**(p. 89)**

Cereal & Breads . . . .**(p. 117)**

So set up this little book on your countertop, flip page after page for some good-eating inspiration and kitchen tips and tricks, and you might just find a little encouragement for your soul along the way. Enjoy!

Main Dishes & Casseroles

They asked for meat, and he sent them quail;
he satisfied their hunger with manna—
bread from heaven.
PSALM 105:40

PORCUPINE MEATBALLS

2 pounds ground beef
2 (11 ounce) cans tomato soup
2½ teaspoons chili powder, divided
Salt and pepper to taste
1 egg
1 medium onion, finely chopped
¼ cup rice (not instant)

....

In skillet, brown ground beef and set aside. Heat soup to boil and then reduce to simmer. With each can of soup, add 2 cans water. Add to soup: 1 teaspoon chili powder and salt and pepper to taste. Let soup mixture simmer while mixing the following ingredients in large bowl: egg, onion, rice, remaining chili powder, and ground beef. Salt and pepper to taste. Mix well and shape into meatballs. Be careful not to pack meatballs too tightly. Drop meatballs into hot soup mixture and bring to boil. Reduce heat and simmer 1½ hours.

HAMBURGER STROGANOFF

1 pound ground beef
½ cup chopped onion
¼ cup butter
2 tablespoons flour
¼ teaspoon pepper
1 teaspoon salt
1 teaspoon garlic salt
1 (8 ounce) can mushrooms (drained)
1 (10½ ounce) can cream of chicken soup
1 cup sour cream
2 cups hot cooked noodles

Heat ground beef, onion, and butter in large skillet on medium-high heat until onion is tender. Stir in flour, pepper, salt, garlic salt, and mushrooms. Cook, stirring constantly, for 5 minutes. Remove from heat and stir in soup. Simmer 10 minutes uncovered. Stir in sour cream and serve over hot noodles.

CRAB ST. LAURENT

MAIN DISHES & CASSEROLES

1 tablespoon butter
1 tablespoon flour
½ cup stock
½ cup cream
½ teaspoon salt
¼ teaspoon pepper
1 cup boiled crabmeat
2 tablespoons grated Parmesan cheese, divided
2 tablespoons white wine vinegar
Buttered toast, cut into fourths
Cayenne pepper to taste

....

Place a saucepan over medium heat with one tablespoon butter. When melted, add flour and stir. Slowly add stock and stir until smooth, then add cream. When thickened, add salt and pepper, crabmeat, and 1½ tablespoons Parmesan cheese. Simmer 2 to 3 minutes and add vinegar. Spread mixture over pieces of buttered toast; sprinkle with remaining Parmesan cheese. Broil toast wedges for 3 minutes, then sprinkle with cayenne pepper to taste.

CHICKEN SPAGHETTI

1 whole chicken, cooked
1 cup diced celery
1 cup diced onion
2 cups chicken broth
1 (10½ ounce) can mushroom soup
1 pound Velveeta cheese, cubed
16 ounces prepared spaghetti
1 small jar pimientos

Debone cooked chicken. In large saucepan, heat celery and onion in chicken broth on medium-high heat for 15 minutes. Reduce heat to medium and stir in soup and cheese until melted. Combine chicken, prepared spaghetti, and pimientos in large casserole dish, then pour hot soup mixture over top. Mix well and bake at 350 degrees for 20 to 30 minutes or until hot and bubbly.

NOT-TOO-HOT CHILI

1 pound ground beef
1 cup chopped onion
4 minced garlic cloves
1 cup chopped green bell pepper
2 (14 ounce) cans diced tomatoes
1 (8 ounce) can tomato sauce
1½ tablespoons chili powder
1 teaspoon salt
¼ teaspoon cayenne pepper
¼ teaspoon paprika
¼ teaspoon cumin
1 (15½ ounce) can kidney beans

....

Brown ground beef with onion, garlic, and bell pepper in large skillet. Drain fat and transfer meat to a slow cooker. Stir in remaining ingredients and cook on high for 2 hours, stirring occasionally. Refrigerate 24 hours. Reheat in microwave or on stovetop. Serve topped with your favorite chili toppings.

PINEAPPLE PORK CHOPS

6 to 8 pork chops
Salt and pepper to taste
Cooking oil
1 (16 ounce) can crushed pineapple (do not drain)
1 cup minute rice

....

Salt and pepper pork chops.
Cover bottom of frying
pan in cooking oil. Brown
chops on each side over
medium heat. Pour crushed
pineapple with juice over
pork chops. Reduce heat
to low, cover, and cook
35 minutes. Slide chops to
one side of frying pan and
pour rice into remaining
pineapple and juice. Add
water if needed. Replace lid
and cook until pork chops
test done.

CORN BREAD PIE

1 pound ground beef
½ cup chopped onion
1 teaspoon salt
¾ teaspoon pepper
1½ cups water
1 (10½ ounce) can tomato soup
1 (12 ounce) can whole kernel corn
1 tablespoon chili powder
½ cup chopped green bell pepper

Topping:
1 egg
½ cup milk
1 tablespoon cooking oil
1½ teaspoons baking powder
¾ cup corn meal
1 tablespoon flour
1 tablespoon sugar

Brown ground beef and onion in frying pan and drain fat. Combine remaining ingredients for corn bread pie. Mix well and simmer 15 minutes. Spray casserole dish with nonstick spray and pour in mixture.

Topping: Combine all topping ingredients in frying pan and stir 2 minutes. Then drop topping mixture on top of casserole mixture. Bake at 350 degrees for 20 minutes.

HANDY CONVERSIONS

1 teaspoon = 5 milliliters
1 tablespoon = 15 milliliters
1 fluid ounce = 30 milliliters
1 cup = 250 milliliters
1 pint = 2 cups (or 16 fluid ounces)
1 quart = 4 cups (or 2 pints or
32 fluid ounces)
1 gallon = 16 cups (or 4 quarts)
1 peck = 8 quarts
1 bushel = 4 pecks
1 pound = 454 grams

Quick Chart

Fahrenheit	Celsius
250°–300°	121°–149°
300°–325°	149°–163°
325°–350°	163°–177°
375°	191°
400°– 425°	204°–218°

GRANDMA G'S MEAT LOAF

1 onion, chopped
1 cup bread crumbs
1 teaspoon salt
½ teaspoon pepper
½ cup milk
1 egg
1 teaspoon sage
1 pound ground beef

Topping:
½ cup catsup
1 teaspoon nutmeg
⅔ cup brown sugar
1 teaspoon mustard

Combine all meat loaf ingredients, except beef, then add beef and mix well. Form into loaf and put in loaf pan. Topping: In bowl, mix all topping ingredients and spread on meat loaf. Bake 1 hour at 350 degrees.

CROCK POT ROAST

2 to 3 pounds pot roast
1½ cups water
1 beef bouillon cube
1 envelope onion soup mix

....

Brown roast in frying pan. Place roast in slow
cooker and cover with water. Add beef bouillon
and soup mix. Cook on high for 3½ to 4 hours or
until roast is falling apart.

PORK & FENNEL RAGU

1 cup finely chopped onion
1 cup finely chopped fennel
2 minced garlic cloves
1 tablespoon fennel seeds
2 teaspoons sugar
1 teaspoon oregano
½ teaspoon salt
½ teaspoon crushed red pepper flakes
¼ teaspoon black pepper
¼ teaspoon ground red pepper
8 ounces lean ground pork
½ cup fat-free, low-sodium chicken broth
2 cups chopped tomato
4 cups hot cooked rigatoni

Heat large skillet coated with cooking spray over medium-high heat. Add onion, fennel, and garlic, and cook 5 minutes. Add fennel seeds, sugar, oregano, salt, red pepper flakes, black pepper, ground red pepper, and pork, stirring to combine. Sauté 3 minutes. Add broth and tomato, and bring to boil. Reduce heat and simmer 15 minutes, stirring occasionally. Serve over hot rigatoni.

HAM LOAF

1 pound chopped or ground ham
1 pound ground pork
2 eggs
1 cup bread crumbs
1 tablespoon chopped green bell pepper
1 tablespoon chopped onion
1/4 teaspoon salt
Flour

Basting Liquid:
2 cups brown sugar
1 teaspoon mustard
1/3 cup crushed pineapple
1/2 cup water
1/3 cup vinegar

Preheat oven to 350 degrees. Combine meats, eggs, bread crumbs, bell pepper, onion, and salt. Form into loaf and place in greased casserole dish. Sprinkle loaf lightly with flour.

Basting Liquid: In saucepan, combine all basting ingredients and bring to boil, stirring constantly for 3 minutes, until mixture thickens. Pour basting liquid over loaf and bake 1 hour, basting often.

BROCCOLI CHEESE RICE

1 cup rice
1 (16 ounce) bag frozen broccoli
1 (10½ ounce) can cream of mushroom soup
1 (10 ounce) jar processed American cheese

Cook rice according to package directions. Steam broccoli in microwave. When both are completely cooked, combine in large bowl. Stir in soup and cheese. Mix thoroughly and serve. Do not add salt.

GRANDPA BLAINE'S GARLIC & CHEESE MASHED POTATOES

10 medium potatoes
½ cup chopped onion
1 tablespoon garlic powder
¾ cup butter
1 cup sour cream
2 cups shredded cheddar cheese
Salt and pepper to taste

....

Peel and chop potatoes and put in large pot of water. Bring potatoes to boil. Add onion and garlic powder. Drain potatoes, removing as much water as possible. Mix in butter and whip potatoes to smooth consistency. Add sour cream and shredded cheddar cheese. Season with salt and pepper to taste.

SKILLET CHICKEN CASSEROLE

4 teaspoons olive oil
1 ½ pounds chicken breasts, boneless and skinless
Salt and pepper to taste
1 small chopped onion
⅓ cup flour
1 cup sliced mushrooms
1 cup milk
1 cup half-and-half
¼ cup chopped parsley
1 (2 ounce) jar diced pimiento
½ teaspoon paprika

Heat olive oil in 12-inch skillet on medium-high heat. Cut chicken breasts into ½-inch cubes and season with salt and pepper. Add cubed chicken to skillet. Cook, stirring, until chicken is golden brown. Add chopped onion and brown. Add flour and sliced mushrooms, stirring constantly. Slowly pour in milk and half-and-half, stirring constantly. Bring mixture to boil and allow to thicken. Remove from heat and stir in parsley. Drain pimiento and add with paprika. Serve.

BEEF TIPS WITH GRAVY

1 pound round steak
2 tablespoons oil
1 envelope onion soup mix
1 (10½ ounce) can cream of mushroom soup

Cut meat into 1½-inch strips; in skillet brown strips in oil over medium-high heat. Mix mushroom soup add onion soup mix with 2 cups water. Add to browned meat and simmer for 1 hour. Serve over noodles or rice.

TIME SAVER

When browning ground beef, brown 3 to 4 pounds at once in a large skillet. Drain off the fat and divide beef evenly in freezer containers and freeze. To use, thaw in the microwave for your next recipe that calls for ground beef.

Quick Tip

SPICY CHICKEN CASSEROLE

1 (10½ ounce) can cream of mushroom soup
1 (10½ ounce) can cream of chicken soup
1 small can tomato sauce
¼ cup water
18 corn tortillas
1 pound Velveeta cheese
6 finely chopped green chilies
1 small onion, chopped
2 large chicken breasts, cooked and chopped

Preheat oven to 350 degrees. In bowl, mix soups and tomato sauce with water. Layer bottom of casserole dish with half the tortillas and top with half the sauce. Cut Velveeta cheese into 1-inch cubes and drop half the cheese, green chilies, and onion over tortillas and sauce. Follow with half the chicken. Repeat layers. Bake 30 minutes.

CHICKEN & RICE

6 chicken breast halves
1 cup fresh mushrooms
1 cup cider vinegar
1 (10½ ounce) can cream of mushroom soup
1 pint sour cream
Dash paprika

Preheat oven to 350 degrees. Debone chicken breast and arrange in baking dish. Bake 15 minutes. Chop mushrooms and combine in bowl with remaining ingredients except paprika. Pour over chicken and bake 30 minutes. Sprinkle with paprika and serve over white rice.

HONEY-LIME PORK CHOPS

½ cup lime juice
¼ cup vegetable oil
½ teaspoon cumin
⅛ teaspoon cayenne pepper
2 tablespoons honey
1 tablespoon Dijon mustard
2 garlic cloves, minced
¼ teaspoon salt
½ teaspoon pepper
6 to 8 pork chops

....

Mix all ingredients except pork chops in large resealable plastic bag. Shake ingredients to mix, then add pork chops. Seal bag and turn to coat pork chops with mixture. Refrigerate overnight. Drain and discard marinade. Grill chops, covered, over medium heat.

SOUTHERN POTATO SALAD

8 large potatoes
4 boiled eggs, diced
2 cups diced red onion
2 cups diced celery
1 pound crispy fried bacon
2 tablespoons mustard
1 cup mayonnaise
4 tablespoons relish
1 teaspoon salt

Peel potatoes and dice into bite-size pieces. Boil in large pot to desired consistency. Drain and cool. Mix all ingredients in large bowl. Refrigerate until cool and serve.

CRAWFISH ÉTOUFFÉE

½ cup butter
2 tablespoons flour
1 large onion, chopped
2 tablespoons minced bell pepper
½ stalk minced celery
2 cloves garlic
1 pound crawfish tails, with fat
2 teaspoons tomato paste
2 cups water
Dash salt
Dash cayenne pepper
Dash pepper
Green onion tops, chopped
Fresh parsley

....

Melt butter in pot, add flour and stir. Add onion, bell pepper, celery, and garlic. Cook until tender, stirring continuously. Add crawfish fat and cook 10 minutes. Add tails and tomato paste, then add water. Cook 20 more minutes. Add salt and both peppers to taste. Cook 5 minutes more and add chopped green onion tops and parsley. Cook an additional 5 minutes.

CHICKEN & DUMPLINGS

1 whole chicken
1 carrot, sliced
2 cloves garlic
1 teaspoon salt
3 large eggs

5 cups flour
1/2 teaspoon baking powder
1/2 teaspoon salt
1 teaspoon pepper

....

In large pot, cover chicken with water and cook with sliced carrot, garlic, and salt. Cook on medium-high heat 2 hours at slow boil until chicken flesh falls away from bone. Allow stock to cool completely. In bowl, whisk eggs with 1 cup cold chicken stock from pot. In separate bowl, mix flour, baking powder, salt, and pepper. Stir stock/egg mixture into flour mixture to form a dough. Knead dough 2 minutes and roll out on floured surface to 1-inch thick. Cut out dumplings and pile on floured plate with flour between each layer. Reheat pot of stock and drop in dumplings and deboned chicken pieces. Cook for 5 minutes and serve.

SHRIMP GUMBO

1 pound pork sausage
4 tablespoons olive oil, divided
2 tablespoons flour
2 pounds medium shrimp, washed and deveined
3 cups chopped okra
2 medium onions, chopped
1 cup chopped celery
2 (14½ ounce) cans diced tomatoes
3 quarts water
2 bay leaves
½ teaspoon cayenne pepper or to taste
1 tablespoon salt
3 cloves minced garlic
½ teaspoon dried thyme
1 chopped red bell pepper
2 cups cooked brown rice

In small skillet, brown sausage and drain off fat, set aside. Make a dark roux by mixing 2 tablespoons oil with the flour together in large skillet; cook on medium heat, browning slowly and stirring frequently. Stir in shrimp. Cook until shrimp turns pink. Set aside. In large pan, heat 2 tablespoons oil over medium heat. Stir in okra, onions, and celery. Cook until okra is tender. Combine tomatoes, water, bay leaves, cayenne pepper, salt, garlic, dried thyme, bell pepper, sausage, and shrimp mixture. Simmer covered for 30 minutes. Add cooked rice and simmer 15 more minutes before serving.

BRAIDED STROMBOLI

2 (1 pound) loaves frozen bread dough,
   thawed and risen
½ cup spaghetti sauce
½ teaspoon dried oregano
4 ounces sliced pepperoni
¼ pound thinly sliced deli ham
¼ pound thinly sliced salami
2 cups shredded mozzarella cheese
2 cups shredded cheddar cheese
⅓ cup grated Parmesan cheese

Preheat oven to 350 degrees. Punch risen dough
down. On lightly floured surface, roll each loaf
into 20x8-inch rectangle. Place 1 rectangle on
greased baking sheet. Spread spaghetti sauce in
wide strip down center. Sprinkle with oregano and
top with pepperoni, ham, salami, mozzarella, and
cheddar. Fold long sides of dough up toward filling;
set aside. Cut remaining rectangle into 3 strips.
Loosely braid strips; pinch ends to seal. Place braid
on top of cheese; pinch braid to dough to seal.
Sprinkle with Parmesan cheese. Bake 30 minutes
or until golden brown.

EASY CLEANUP

To easily remove burned food from a skillet, add a drop or two of dish soap and enough water to cover the bottom of the pan. Then set it on the stove and bring the soapy water to a boil to remove the offending foods.

INCREDIBLE BREAKFAST CASSEROLE

12 to 16 ounces sausage
½ to 1 cup chopped onion
1 small can diced potatoes
8 large eggs
1½ cups milk
Salt and pepper to taste
5 slices bread, torn into 1-inch pieces
2 cups shredded cheddar cheese, divided

Preheat oven to 350 degrees. Butter 2-quart baking dish. In large skillet, cook sausage with onion and potatoes. Whisk eggs with milk in bowl and season with salt and pepper; set aside. Arrange torn bread in bottom of baking dish. Sprinkle with sausage mixture and top with half the cheddar cheese. Pour egg mixture evenly over top and sprinkle with remaining cheese. Bake 35 to 40 minutes, until puffy and lightly browned.

Soups, Salads & Vegetables

A bowl of vegetables with someone you love is better than steak with someone you hate.
PROVERBS 15:17

CRUNCHY CABBAGE SALAD

1 head Napa cabbage, finely sliced
5 green onions, thinly sliced

Dressing:
1 cup sugar
½ cup cider vinegar
2 tablespoons soy sauce
1 package Ramen noodles seasoning (chicken)

Topping:
⅓ cup butter
½ cup sliced almonds
2 tablespoons sesame seeds
Noodles from Ramen package, crushed

In large bowl combine Napa cabbage and green onions. Refrigerate until ready for use. Dressing: Mix all ingredients in a jar and set aside, but periodically shake jar until sugar is completely dissolved. Topping: Melt butter in skillet. Add almonds, sesame seeds, and crushed noodles. Fry until golden brown, stirring continually. Before serving, add topping to cabbage/onion mixture, and pour dressing over all. Mix well.

WHITE CHICKEN CHILI SOUP

1 tablespoon vegetable oil
1 (12½ ounce) can chunk chicken breast
  (do not drain in water)
1 package white chicken chili seasoning mix
1 cup water
1 (15 ounce) can white beans (do not drain)
1 (14½ ounce) stewed tomatoes
1 small can diced tomatoes
1 (8¾ ounce) can southwestern-style corn

Heat oil in large skillet on medium-high heat. Add chicken and stir for 5 minutes or until brown. Stir in seasoning mix, water, beans, tomatoes, and corn. Bring to boil. Reduce heat to low; cover and simmer 10 minutes.

HOT TACO SOUP

2 pounds ground beef
1 large onion, chopped
1 (15 ounce) can pinto beans
1 can whole kernel corn (drained)
1 can Mexican-style stewed tomatoes
1 can diced tomatoes
1 package taco seasoning mix
1 envelope ranch dressing mix
2½ cups water

....

Brown ground beef and onions in large pan, drain fat. Add remaining ingredients and simmer for 1½ hours.

FRIED CABBAGE

2 tablespoons vegetable oil
3 cups shredded cabbage
1 cup chopped green bell pepper
½ teaspoon salt
Dash pepper
2 cups fresh diced tomatoes
½ cup chopped onion
½ teaspoon sugar
1 cup chopped celery

Heat vegetable oil in frying pan and add all ingredients. Cook 10 minutes or until vegetables are tender.

GRAPE SALAD

½ cup granulated sugar
1 cup cream cheese
1 cup sour cream
2 pounds red grapes
2 pounds green grapes
1 cup brown sugar, packed
1 cup pecans, chopped

Cream together granulated sugar, cream cheese, and sour cream. In large bowl, stir creamed mixture into grapes. Combine brown sugar and pecans and sprinkle on grape mixture. Refrigerate 1 hour before serving.

SAUSAGE LENTIL STEW

½ pound bulk Italian sausage
1 large onion, finely chopped
1 small green bell pepper, finely chopped
1 small carrot, grated or finely chopped
1 large garlic clove, minced
1 bay leaf
2 (14½ ounce) cans chicken broth
1 (14½ ounce) can coarsely chopped tomatoes,
  with liquid
1 cup water
¾ cup dry lentils

....

Brown and drain sausage. Combine all ingredients
in large saucepan and simmer for 1 hour. Remove
bay leaf and serve.

FRIED EGGPLANT

1 eggplant
1 quart water
1 tablespoon salt
1 egg
Bread crumbs
Butter or oil

....

Peel and cut eggplant into thin slices; lay slices in bowl. Mix water with salt; pour over eggplant. You can put a small plate on top of slices to keep them under salt water. Soak in water at least 3 hours. When ready to cook, remove eggplant slices from bowl and dry slices with paper towel. Beat egg in bowl. Dip eggplant slices in egg and then cover with bread crumbs. In skillet, fry eggplant in butter or oil.

PICKLE JUICE POWER

Use leftover dill pickle juice to clean the copper bottoms of your pans. Just pour the juice in a large bowl, and soak the pan in the juice for about 15 minutes. Your copper pans come out looking like new!

.... **Quick Tip** ....

BROCCOLI SALAD

2 heads broccoli
½ cup red onion, chopped
½ cup golden raisins
⅓ cup chopped pecans
10 slices bacon, fried and crumbled
2 cups Thousand Island dressing

. . . .

Chop broccoli, including stems, into bite-size pieces. In large bowl, toss all ingredients together with dressing and serve immediately, or chill in refrigerator up to 24 hours.

LEMON-LIME SODA SALAD

1 package lemon gelatin mix
1 cup boiling water
1 (8 ounce) package cream cheese, softened
1 teaspoon sugar
1 teaspoon vanilla
3 drops green food coloring
1 cup canned pineapple (drained)
10 ounces lemon-lime soda
½ cup chopped nuts

....

Dissolve gelatin mix in boiling water. Add cream cheese and beat. Fold in sugar, vanilla, and green food coloring. Add drained pineapple, lemon-lime soda, and nuts. Stir after mixture thickens to keep nuts from floating to the top.

STUFFED PEPPERS

4 medium green bell peppers
I pound ground beef
2 cups cooked rice
¼ cup chopped onion
I½ teaspoons salt
¼ teaspoon pepper
I (15 ounce) can tomato sauce, divided
I cup shredded cheddar cheese

Preheat oven to 350 degrees. Wash bell peppers and slice in half lengthwise. Remove seeds. Combine beef, rice, onion, salt, pepper, and ½ cup tomato sauce. Fill pepper halves with mixture and place in shallow baking dish. Pour remaining tomato sauce over peppers. Cover and bake 50 minutes. Remove cover and spoon cheese on top of each pepper. Bake uncovered an additional 10 minutes.

CHEESY CREAM CORN

1 (8 ounce) package shredded cheddar cheese
2 (8 ounce) packages cream cheese
3 pounds frozen corn
¼ cup butter or margarine
3 tablespoons milk
1 small can green chilies
3 tablespoons water

Mix all ingredients in slow cooker. Cook 4 hours, until bubbly.

PASTA VEGGIE SOUP

2 teaspoons olive oil
6 cloves garlic, minced
1½ cups shredded carrots
1 cup chopped onion
1 cup celery, thinly sliced
4 cups chicken broth
4 cups water
1½ cups uncooked ditalini pasta
¼ cup shaved Parmesan cheese

In 6-quart Dutch oven, heat oil over medium heat. Add garlic and stir for 15 seconds. Add carrots, onion, and celery and cook 5 minutes until tender, stirring constantly. Add chicken broth and water and bring to boil. Add pasta and cook 7 to 10 minutes until pasta is tender. Top each serving with Parmesan cheese.

POTATOES AU GRATIN

6 large boiled potatoes
2 tablespoons butter
2 tablespoons flour
4 tablespoons sharp cheddar cheese, grated
½ pint milk
½ pint chicken broth
4 egg yolks
Salt and pepper to taste
¼ cup bread crumbs

Preheat oven to 350 degrees. Cut potatoes into thin slices and set aside. In saucepan over medium heat, combine butter, flour, cheese, milk, and chicken broth; stir till mixture resembles sauce. Remove from heat and add egg yolks, salt, and pepper. Alternate layers of potatoes and sauce in 9x9-inch baking dish, starting with potatoes and ending with sauce. Sprinkle top with bread crumbs. Bake 20 minutes until bubbly.

SUCCOTASH

1 cup sweet corn
2 cups string beans, cut into 2-inch pieces
1 cup lima beans
Salt and pepper to taste
1 tablespoon butter
⅛ cup brown-rice flour

Place corn, string beans, and lima beans in large saucepan. Add enough water to cover vegetables, and put on medium-high heat to boil. Add salt and pepper to taste. When beans are tender, add butter and a little more salt and pepper. Thicken mixture with brown-rice flour.

TOMATO PIE

1 (9 inch) frozen pie shell
3 cups chopped tomatoes
1 cup chopped yellow onion
¼ cup sliced basil
2 cups grated cheese (combination of sharp cheddar and Monterey Jack, Gruyère, or mozzarella)
¾ cup mayonnaise
1 teaspoon Tabasco sauce
Salt and pepper to taste

....

Preheat oven to 350 degrees. Place pie shell in oven and bake 10 minutes or until lightly golden. Squeeze as much moisture as possible out of chopped tomatoes, using paper towels, a clean dish towel, or a potato ricer. Sprinkle chopped onion in cooked pie shell. Spread chopped tomatoes over onions. Sprinkle sliced basil on tomatoes. In medium bowl, mix together grated cheese, mayonnaise, Tabasco, and salt and pepper to taste. Spread cheese mixture on top of pie. Place in oven and bake until browned and bubbly, 30 to 45 minutes.

CRISPER LETTUCE

Lettuce remains fresh longer if you store it in the refrigerator without washing it. Keep the leaves dry and wash lettuce right before you use it. Store lettuce in paper bags rather than plastic in the crisper and it will stay fresher longer.

Quick Tip

CORN CHIP SALAD

1 can ranch-style beans
1 small head lettuce
2 tomatoes
1 small onion
½ pound grated cheddar cheese
½ bottle Catalina salad dressing
1 pound corn chips, crushed

Drain and rinse beans. Chop lettuce, tomatoes, and onion. In large bowl, toss all ingredients except corn chips and salad dressing together. Chill in refrigerator at least 15 minutes. Pour salad dressing over salad and add crushed corn chips immediately before serving.

GRANDMA JO'S EVERYDAY BEANS

2 cups dry pinto beans
½ pound ham hock
2 tablespoons chili powder
1 tablespoon dry mustard
1 tablespoon sugar
2 tablespoons molasses
1 chopped onion
Dash salt

Sort and wash beans, and put in large pot. Cover with cold water and soak overnight. Using the same water, add remaining ingredients and cook until beans are tender. Add hot water as needed during cooking.

APPLE AND NUT SALAD

4 tablespoons vinegar
2 eggs
1 heaping teaspoon butter
1 teaspoon mustard
Dash salt
1/4 teaspoon red and white pepper
1 teaspoon sugar
3/4 cup whipped topping
1/2 cup chopped apples
1/2 cup chopped walnuts

In saucepan, let vinegar come to boil; stir in eggs until mixture thickens. Cool. Stir in butter, mustard, salt, pepper, and sugar. Add whipped topping before serving and fold in apples and walnuts.

CRANBERRY SALAD

1 bag cranberries
1 cup sugar
1 bag mini marshmallows
1 cup chopped nuts
1 (8 ounce) container whipped topping

Crush cranberries in blender. In bowl, combine crushed cranberries and sugar; mix well. Marinate in refrigerator for 2 hours. Fold in marshmallows, nuts, and whipped topping. Refrigerate.

STRAWBERRY CHICKEN SALAD

1 (13 ounce) can chunk chicken breast (drained)
1 heaping tablespoon mayonnaise
1 pint fresh strawberries
½ cup shaved almonds

....

In bowl, mix chicken with mayonnaise. Wash
strawberries and slice into bite-size pieces
over bowl with chicken in it so that all juice
from strawberries drips into salad. Drop in
strawberries. Pour in almonds. Stir and serve with
crackers.

RASPBERRY SPINACH SALAD

5 ounces spinach
1/2 medium-size sliced red onion
1 1/2 cup raspberries
1/2 cup blue cheese or crumbled feta
1 cup honey-roasted walnuts
2 tablespoons red raspberry vinegar
3 tablespoons olive oil
Salt and pepper to taste

....

Combine spinach, sliced red onion, raspberries, crumbled cheese, and honey-roasted walnuts in salad bowl. In separate small bowl, whisk raspberry vinegar, olive oil, and salt and pepper to taste until well blended. Add the raspberry vinaigrette to salad and toss well. Serve immediately.

GARDEN-RIPE PARMESAN TOMATOES

2 large, very ripe tomatoes
Vinegar and oil mixture
Parmesan cheese
Sliced cucumbers
Celery sticks

Slice tomatoes into ¼-inch slices. Lightly cover with vinegar and oil. Sprinkle with Parmesan cheese and serve with sliced cucumbers and celery sticks.

STEAK SOUP

1½ pounds ground chuck
½ cup chopped onion
2 tablespoons butter or margarine
1 cup flour
6 cups water
1 tablespoon browning sauce (such as Kitchen Bouquet or Gravy Master)
3 beef bouillon cubes
2 (10 ounce) packages frozen mixed vegetables
1 stalk celery, chopped
1 (11 ounce) can tomatoes

In large pot, brown meat and chopped onion in butter. Stir in flour and gradually add water, browning sauce, and bouillon. Add mixed vegetables, celery, and tomatoes. Slow cook on low heat on stove for 2½ hours, stirring often.

SALTY SOUP

If your soup has been oversalted, cut up a
raw potato or two and drop into the pot.
The potato will absorb some of the salt.

CRUNCHY COLESLAW

1 medium head cabbage
1 bunch green onions
2 packages Ramen noodles
½ cup butter or margarine
1 cup almonds
½ cup sesame seeds

Dressing:
1 cup canola oil
1 cup sugar
½ cup white vinegar
1 tablespoon soy sauce

Slice cabbage and green onions thinly and chill in bowl. Discard seasoning packets from Ramen noodles and crush noodles in package. In skillet, melt butter, then brown Ramen noodles, almonds, and sesame seeds. Set aside. Dressing: Mix all ingredients and keep at room temperature. To serve: Toss skillet ingredients with chilled cabbage mixture and add dressing. Mix well.

Cakes, Cookies & Sweets

Kind words are like honey—sweet to the soul and healthy for the body.
PROVERBS 16:24

CINNAMON BROWNIES

1 cup butter
1 cup water
2 eggs
½ cup milk
2 cups flour
2 cups sugar
2 heaping teaspoons cinnamon
1 heaping teaspoon baking soda
4 tablespoons cocoa
1 teaspoon vanilla

Frosting:
½ cup butter
6 tablespoons milk
1 pound powdered sugar
4 tablespoons cocoa
1 cup chopped pecans
1 teaspoon vanilla

Preheat oven to 400 degrees. Bring butter and water to boil in small saucepan. In small bowl, beat eggs and milk. In large mixing bowl, combine dry ingredients. Stir egg mixture into dry ingredients and mix well. Slowly stir in hot butter and water mixture a little at a time so as not to cook eggs. Add vanilla and pour into greased jellyroll pan. Bake 20 minutes or until brownies test done. Frosting: Bring butter and milk to boil. Stir in remaining ingredients. Spread over warm brownies.

AMAZING PUDDING

1 can crushed pineapple
2 (3 ounce) boxes pistachio-flavor instant
    pudding mix
1 container small-curd cottage cheese
1 (8 ounce) container whipped topping

Drain pineapple, reserving juice. In large bowl,
combine all ingredients. Add pineapple juice to
desired consistency. Mixture should be thick.
Refrigerate for several hours. Serve cold.

PEANUT CLUSTERS

½ pound milk chocolate
⅔ cup sweetened condensed milk
1 cup unsalted peanuts

....

Use double boiler to melt chocolate. Remove from heat and stir in sweetened condensed milk. Add peanuts, and mix until peanuts are well covered. Drop by spoonfuls onto greased cookie sheet. Refrigerate 3 hours, then serve.

CHERRIES IN THE SNOW

½ cup butter
½ cup brown sugar
2 cups flour
1 cup chopped pecans
1 (8 ounce) package cream cheese
2 tablespoons vanilla
1 cup powdered sugar
1 (8 ounce) container whipped topping
1 (15 ounce) can cherry pie filling

....

Preheat oven to 350 degrees. Melt butter and mix in bowl with brown sugar, flour, and pecans. Pat mixture lightly into 9x13-inch baking pan. Bake 20 minutes and let cool 5 minutes. In bowl, combine cream cheese, vanilla, powdered sugar, and whipped topping. Spread over warm crust. Top with cherry pie filling and refrigerate. Serve chilled.

PUMPKIN BREAD

2 cups sugar
5 eggs
1 ½ cups vegetable oil
1 (14 ounce) can pumpkin purée
2 cups flour
1 teaspoon baking soda
1 teaspoon cinnamon
1 teaspoon salt
1 teaspoon nutmeg
1 teaspoon allspice
2 (3 ounce) boxes vanilla instant pudding mix

Preheat oven to 350 degrees. In large bowl, combine sugar, eggs, oil, and pumpkin. In another bowl, mix flour, baking soda, cinnamon, salt, nutmeg, allspice, and pudding mix. Combine dry ingredients with pumpkin mixture and stir in pecans. Pour into ungreased loaf pans. Bake 40 minutes.

DUMP CAKE

1 cup butter
1 large can crushed pineapple (do not drain)
1 (15 ounce) can cherry pie filling
1 box yellow cake mix
2 cups chopped nuts
Whipped cream

....

Preheat oven to 325 degrees. In small saucepan, melt butter and pour into 9x13-inch baking pan. Dump pineapple with juice into baking pan, then pie filling, then cake mix, and finally nuts, spreading out each layer evenly. Bake 1 hour or until cherry pie filling oozes through other ingredients and nuts are brown. Serve with whipped cream.

COCONUT CUSTARD WITH CRUST

5 eggs
½ cup sugar
2 cups milk
½ cup flour
1 cup coconut
2 tablespoons butter
2 teaspoons vanilla

....

Preheat oven to 350 degrees. In large bowl, mix all ingredients together. Pour into greased deep-dish pie pan. Bake 45 minutes and allow to cool. It should fall a little.

NUTS ABOUT CAKE

If your cake recipe calls for nuts, heat them first in the oven, then dust with flour before adding to the batter to keep them from settling to the bottom of the pan.

Quick Tip

4 cups chopped apples
1 cup sugar
½ teaspoon cinnamon
3 tablespoons flour
½ cup salt

Topping:
½ cup rolled oats
½ cup flour
½ cup brown sugar
⅓ cup melted butter

Preheat oven to 350 degrees. In bowl, mix together apples, sugar, cinnamon, flour, and salt and transfer to baking dish. Topping: Mix together oats, flour, brown sugar, and melted butter and pour over apple mixture. Bake 40 minutes.

STRAWBERRY JELL-O CAKE

CAKES, COOKIES & SWEETS

½ cup water
1 (3 ounce) package strawberry gelatin mix
1 box white cake mix
1 cup vegetable oil
4 eggs
3 tablespoons flour
1 cup strawberries (fresh or frozen)

Frosting:
½ cup softened butter
1 pound powdered sugar
⅓ cup strawberries

Preheat oven to 350 degrees. Bring water to boil. Stir in gelatin mix and set aside. In separate bowl, combine cake mix and oil. Mix until smooth. Add eggs and flour. Mix until smooth again. Add gelatin and strawberries. Pour into greased 9x13-inch baking pan. Bake 35 minutes or until cake tests done. Frosting: Blend softened butter, powdered sugar, and strawberries until smooth. Frost cooled cake.

ORANGE BALLS

1 (6 ounce) can frozen orange juice concentrate
½ cup butter
1 box vanilla wafers
1 pound powdered sugar
Coconut flakes

....

Allow frozen juice to thaw to slushy state. Melt
butter. Crush vanilla wafers. In large bowl, mix all
ingredients (except coconut) together and form
mixture into walnut-size balls. Roll balls in flaked
coconut and set on baking sheet. Refrigerate until
ready to serve.

OLD-FASHIONED APPLE PIE

Pastry dough for a double crust pie
8 cups pared, sliced tart baking apples
1 cup sugar
2 tablespoons flour
1 teaspoon cinnamon
½ teaspoon nutmeg
¼ teaspoon salt
½ teaspoon grated lemon rind
2 to 3 teaspoons fresh lemon juice
2 tablespoon butter
1 egg yolk
1 tablespoon water

Roll out half of pastry dough and place in a 9-inch deep dish pie pan. Preheat oven to 425 degrees. Combine apple slices, sugar, flour, cinnamon, nutmeg, salt, lemon rind, and lemon juice in large bowl. Turn into pie plate. Dot with butter. Roll out remaining half of pastry dough. Cut into strips. Place on top of apples making crisscross with strips. Brush with egg yolk mixed with water. Bake for 40 to 45 minutes. Remove from oven and cool on rack. Serve warm or room temperature.

ICE BOX DESSERT

¾ cup butter
1 cup chopped pecans
1½ cups flour
1 cup powdered sugar
1 (8 ounce) package cream cheese, softened
1 (8 ounce) container whipped topping, divided
1 (3 ounce) box vanilla instant pudding mix
1 (3 ounce) box of your favorite flavor instant
   pudding mix
3 cups milk

Preheat oven to 350 degrees. Melt butter and combine in bowl with pecans and flour. Press into 9x13-inch greased baking pan. Bake 10 minutes, or until lightly browned. Cool. In bowl, cream together powdered sugar and cream cheese. Fold in 1 cup whipped topping, and spoon over cooled crust. In another bowl combine both boxes of instant pudding mix and milk. Mix well and pour over cream cheese mixture. Top with remaining whipped topping. Refrigerate several hours before serving.

CREAM CHEESE BARS

1 box lemon cake mix
½ cup butter
3 eggs, divided
1 (8 ounce) package cream cheese
1 package lemon frosting mix

....

Preheat oven to 350 degrees. In bowl, combine cake mix, butter, and 1 egg and stir until moist. Press mixture into greased 9x13-inch baking dish. In separate bowl, mix cream cheese and frosting mix until smooth. Set aside ½ cup of this mixture for topping. To remaining cream cheese mixture add 2 eggs and beat 4 minutes. Spread onto cake mixture and bake 35 minutes. Let cool and then spread the ½ cup reserved frosting mixture (add in a little water if mixture has become stiff) over top.

GRANDMA SPENCER'S GRAHAM CRACKER PUDDING

2 (3 ounce) boxes vanilla instant pudding mix
1 box graham crackers
2 (21 ounce) cans cherry pie filling

Mix pudding according to package directions and let set 5 minutes. Layer graham crackers in bottom of 9x13-inch baking pan. Layer half of pudding on top of graham cracker layer. Pour half of cherry pie filling onto vanilla pudding. Continue with layers: another layer of graham crackers, remaining vanilla pudding, remaining cherry pie filling. Refrigerate several hours before serving.

CONFETTI COOKIES

1 cup butter
1 cup brown sugar, packed
1 cup granulated sugar
2 eggs
2 teaspoons vanilla
2¼ cups flour
1 teaspoon baking soda
1 cup multicolored candy-coated chocolate pieces

Preheat oven to 375 degrees. In large bowl, stir all ingredients together and drop onto ungreased baking sheet. Bake 10 minutes. Let cool.

PERFECT BREAD CRUST

When baking bread, a small dish of water in the oven will help keep the crust from getting too hard or brown.

Quick Tip

SUPER QUICK POUND CAKE

1 box vanilla pudding pound cake mix
1 cup flour
1 cup sour cream
1 cup sweet milk
4 eggs
¾ cup sugar
½ teaspoon vanilla
½ teaspoon butter
½ teaspoon almond extract
½ teaspoon lemon extract

Preheat oven to 350 degrees. Combine all ingredients in large mixing bowl and beat 2 minutes. Pour into greased pound cake baking pan. Bake 1 hour and 10 minutes. Cool 5 minutes in pan.

GRAMPS'S MICROWAVE PEANUT BRITTLE

1 cup sugar
½ cup light corn syrup
1 cup raw peanuts
⅛ teaspoon salt
1 tablespoon butter
1 teaspoon vanilla
1 teaspoon baking soda

Combine sugar, corn syrup, peanuts, and salt in 2-quart microwavable mixing bowl. Microwave on high 8 minutes, stirring after 4 minutes. Add butter. Microwave on high 2 minutes. Brittle should not get too brown. Stir in vanilla and baking soda until light and foamy. Spread on buttered baking sheet as thinly as possible. Cool. Break into pieces.

MISSISSIPPI MUD CAKE

3 tablespoons cocoa
2 cups sugar
1 cup butter
1 teaspoon vanilla
4 eggs
1½ cups flour
1⅓ cups coconut
1 cups chopped
   pecans, divided
1 large jar marshmallow
   crème

Frosting:
½ cup cocoa
½ cup evaporated milk
1 teaspoon vanilla
1 pound powdered
   sugar
½ cup butter

Preheat oven to 350 degrees. In large bowl, cream cocoa, sugar, and butter. Add vanilla and eggs and mix well. Add flour, coconut, and ½ cup pecans. Beat for 2 minutes. Bake in greased 9x13-inch baking dish for 35 to 40 minutes. While cake is still hot, gently spread marshmallow crème over top and let cool. Frosting: In bowl, beat together cocoa, evaporated milk, vanilla, powdered sugar, and butter until smooth and spread over marshmallow creme. Sprinkle remaining chopped pecans over top.

PEACH FOLDOVERS

1 (10 ounce) can refrigerator biscuits
⅔ cup sugar
¾ teaspoon cinnamon
¼ teaspoon nutmeg
1¼ cups fresh peaches, peeled and chopped
¼ cup butter

....

Preheat oven to 375 degrees. Roll out dough from two biscuits each into 4-inch circles. In small bowl, stir sugar, cinnamon, and nutmeg together. Place 2 tablespoons chopped peaches onto one side of each dough circle. Sprinkle 1 teaspoon sugar mixture over peaches. Fold dough in half. Use fork to seal edges. Melt butter then dip each foldover in butter and then in remaining sugar mixture. Bake on ungreased cookie sheet 15 to 20 minutes.

FUDGE DROPS

1 cup semisweet chocolate chips, divided
3 tablespoons canola oil
1 cup packed brown sugar
3 egg whites
2 tablespoons plus 1½ teaspoons light corn syrup
1 tablespoon water
2½ teaspoons vanilla
1¾ cups flour
⅔ cup plus 1 tablespoon powdered sugar, divided
⅓ cup baking cocoa
2¼ teaspoons baking powder
⅛ teaspoon salt

Preheat oven to 350 degrees. In bowl, combine ¾ cup chocolate chips with oil and melt in microwave; stir until smooth. Pour into large bowl; cool 5 minutes. Stir in brown sugar. Add egg whites, corn syrup, water, and vanilla, and stir until smooth. In separate bowl, combine flour, ⅔ cup powdered sugar, cocoa, baking powder, and salt; gradually add to chocolate mixture until combined. Stir in remaining chocolate chips (dough will be very stiff). Drop by tablespoonfuls 2 inches apart onto greased baking sheets. Bake 10 minutes or until puffed and set. Cool 2 minutes; move to wire racks. Sprinkle cooled cookies with powdered sugar.

RICE PUDDING

1 cup rice, uncooked
2 quarts milk, divided
8 tablespoons sugar
1 teaspoon salt
1 heaping teaspoonful butter, melted
Nutmeg to taste
Cinnamon to taste
Raisins to taste

....

Preheat oven to 300 degrees. Wash rice and soak in 1 pint milk for 2 hours. Then add remaining milk, sugar, salt, butter, nutmeg, cinnamon, and raisins. Pour into 2½-quart baking dish. Bake 2 hours. Let cool and serve cold.

CHOCOLATE CRUNCH CUPCAKES

4 squares semisweet baking chocolate
1 teaspoon vanilla
1 cup chopped nuts of choice
4 large eggs, beaten
1 cup butter
1 cup flour
1¾ cups sugar

Preheat oven to 325 degrees. Melt chocolate in saucepan. Add vanilla and nuts. In bowl, mix together beaten eggs, butter, flour, and sugar. Carefully add to chocolate mixture. Pour into paper liners set in muffin pans and bake 35 minutes.

SWEET POTATO PUDDING

2 cups baked cold sweet potatoes
½ pound sugar
½ pound butter
6 eggs, separated
2 tablespoons apple juice
2 teaspoons vanilla
Juice and zest of 1 lemon
½ teaspoon cinnamon
Dash allspice
Dash ginger
Dash nutmeg

Preheat oven to 250 degrees. Mash cold sweet potatoes through a sieve and set aside in large bowl. In separate bowl, beat sugar, butter, and egg yolks into a cream. Add apple juice, vanilla, juice and zest of lemon, cinnamon, allspice, ginger, and nutmeg. Stir mixture into potato pulp. Fold in egg whites beaten to a froth. Pour into buttered baking dish. Bake 45 minutes.

NO WASTE PASTRY

Whenever you have pastry scraps left after making a piecrust, brush on a little butter, sprinkle with cinnamon and sugar, and bake at 350 degrees for 8 to 10 minutes for a tasty treat that's great with tea!

Quick Tip

QUICK BLACKBERRY COBBLER

½ cup flour
¼ cup butter, softened
¼ cup rolled oats
½ cup brown sugar, divided
2 cups fresh blackberries

....

Preheat oven to 350 degrees. In small bowl, mix flour, butter, oats, and ¼ cup brown sugar until crumbly. Toss berries with remaining brown sugar. Pour berries into greased 8-inch round cake pan. Top with crumble mixture. Bake to bubbling, about 30 minutes.

Appetizers & Beverages

"Anyone who believes in me may come and drink! For the scriptures declare, 'Rivers of living water will flow from his heart.'"
JOHN 7:38

FRUITFUL PIZZA

1 can refrigerated sugar cookie dough
1 package cream cheese
⅓ cup sugar
½ teaspoon vanilla
Fresh fruit, cut into small pieces (bananas,
    apples, mandarin oranges, strawberries,
    peaches, pineapple, kiwi)
2 tablespoons orange marmalade
½ teaspoon water

Preheat oven to 375 degrees. Slice cookie dough
and lay slices on pizza pan. Flatten and spread
slices to completely cover pan with dough.
Bake 12 minutes. Let cool. In bowl, mix cream
cheese, sugar, and vanilla. Spread mixture onto
cooled dough. Arrange fruit on top. Mix orange
marmalade with water and pour glaze over fruit.
Chill, and cut into pizza slices.

HOT PICKLES

1 gallon hamburger dill pickles
5 pounds sugar
1 (2 ounce) jar Tabasco sauce with garlic

....

Drain juice from dill pickles and add sugar to
pickle jar. All of sugar won't fit into jar at once,
so just keep adding slowly until it is all in jar. Add
Tabasco sauce. Leave at room temperature. Turn
jar daily for 10 days. Then serve.

PINK LADY PUNCH

1 ½ cups sugar
2 liters lemon-lime soda
1 quart cranberry juice
1 quart pineapple juice
Drop of red food coloring (optional)

....

In large bowl, dissolve sugar in soda. Mix in juices. Add drop of red food coloring, if desired, and stir well. Freeze in gallon-size freezer bags. When ready to use, thaw till slushy. Serve.

ZUCCHINI BAKE

3 cups chopped zucchini
¾ cup chopped onion
1½ cups biscuit mix
Salt and pepper to taste
½ cup vegetable oil
6 eggs

. . . .

Preheat oven to 350 degrees. Grease 9x13-inch
baking pan. In large bowl, mix all ingredients.
Spread mixture into pan. Bake 40 minutes, until
golden brown. Cut into 2x2-inch squares and
serve at room temperature.

PUFFED CORN

½ pound butter (do not substitute)
1 cup brown sugar
½ cup light corn syrup
2 bags microwave popcorn, popped

∙∙

Preheat oven to 275 degrees. In saucepan, bring butter, brown sugar, and corn syrup to boil and let boil for 3 minutes. Put popcorn in large bowl. Pour sugar mixture over popcorn and mix to coat well. Spread on cookie sheets and bake 45 minutes, stirring every 10 minutes. Break apart when cool and store in airtight containers.

BANANA SLUSH PUNCH

6 cups water
4 cups sugar
5 cups mashed bananas
1 (46 ounce) can orange juice
1 (46 ounce) can pineapple juice
½ cup lemon juice
2 liters ginger ale, chilled

....

Bring water and sugar to boil. Cool, then add bananas, orange juice, pineapple juice, and lemon juice. Freeze in gallon-size freezer bags. Before serving, remove from freezer and let thaw till slushy. Add chilled ginger ale and serve immediately.

AVOCADO TREAT

Avocado
Lemon juice
Chili powder
Salt
Lemon pepper
Garlic salt
Tabasco sauce
Mayonnaise
Saltine crackers

Peel avocado and slice in thin slices. Fan slices out on small plate. Squeeze lemon juice over arrangement, then sprinkle all dry spices onto avocado slices to taste. Drop on Tabasco to taste. Spread mayonnaise on crackers and top with prepped avocado.

QUICK TEA FLAVORINGS

For tea flavoring, dissolve old-fashioned lemon drops or hard mint candy in your tea. They melt fast and keep the tea brisk.

Quick Tip

HOT SPICED TEA

½ cup brown sugar
7 cups water, divided
1 teaspoon pumpkin pie spice
2 cans cranberry sauce
¼ cup lemon juice
1 (12 ounce) can frozen orange juice concentrate

....

Mix brown sugar, 1 cup water, and spice mix in saucepan. Heat to boiling over high heat, stirring constantly, until sugar is dissolved. Remove from heat. Stir in cranberry sauce and mix well. Stir in remaining water, lemon juice, and orange juice concentrate. Return saucepan to stove and heat mixture to boiling. Reduce heat and let simmer uncovered 5 minutes.

TORTILLA ROLLS

4 green onions
1 jalapeño pepper
½ can black olives
1 tablespoon mayonnaise
1 (8 ounce) package cream cheese
1 package soft tortillas

Chop green onions, jalapeño, and olives and place in bowl. Add mayonnaise and cream cheese; blend well. Spread thin layer on each tortilla. Roll up. Refrigerate 30 minutes. Cut rolls into ½-inch slices and place slices on serving plate.

BACON CURRY COLESLAW

½ cup mayonnaise
1 tablespoon vinegar
1 teaspoon sugar
½ teaspoon curry powder
3 cups shredded cabbage
¼ cup raisins
2 tablespoons sliced green onions
4 slices bacon, cooked and crumbled
¼ cup salted peanuts

In bowl, mix mayonnaise, vinegar, sugar, and curry powder. Cover and chill. In separate bowl, combine cabbage, raisins, and green onions; cover and chill. Just before serving, combine cabbage mixture, bacon crumbles, and peanuts in large bowl. Add mayonnaise mixture and toss well.

PURPLE PUNCH

1 large can pineapple juice
2 cups grape juice
1 ½ gallons pineapple sherbet
2 liters ginger ale

In pitcher mix pineapple juice and grape juice.
Remove sherbet from container and lay block of
frozen sherbet in punch bowl 30 minutes before
serving. Pour ginger ale over sherbet to make
foam. Then slowly pour pineapple and grape juice
mixture into bowl.

MEXICAN COFFEE

¾ cup ground dark roast coffee
3 teaspoons ground cinnamon
6 cups water
1 cup milk
⅓ cup chocolate syrup
2 tablespoons light brown sugar
1 teaspoon vanilla
Whipped topping

....

Place coffee and cinnamon in filter basket of coffeemaker. Pour water in machine and brew coffee. In saucepan, blend milk, chocolate syrup, and brown sugar. Stir over low heat until sugar dissolves. Combine milk mixture with brewed coffee in pot and stir in vanilla. Garnish servings with whipped topping and sprinkle with additional cinnamon.

LOADED SOUR CREAM DIP

2 cups light sour cream
1 envelope ranch dressing mix
2 cups real bacon bits
½ cup chopped red or green onions
2 cups shredded cheddar cheese

· ·

In large bowl, combine sour cream with ranch
dressing mix. Add remaining ingredients and
mix well. Cover and refrigerate at least 30
minutes. Serve with your favorite chips or on top
of baked potatoes.

HOT CHOCOLATE MIX

1 (8 quart) box powdered milk
1 (2 pound) box powdered chocolate milk mix
1 (6 ounce) jar powdered cream
⅓ cup powdered sugar
1 teaspoon salt

....

In large bowl, mix all ingredients well and store in airtight container. To make hot chocolate, add ½ cup of dry mix to 8 ounces hot water; stir.

WASSAIL

2 quarts apple cider
2 (14 ounce) cans pineapple juice
2 cups orange juice
1 cup lemon juice
1 stick whole cinnamon
1 teaspoon whole cloves
1 cup sugar

Combine all ingredients in large pot and simmer
5 minutes. Strain and refrigerate overnight. Reheat
and serve warm.

JAR OPENER

If you have a jar that's just too hard to open, try using latex dishwashing gloves. They have a nonslip grip that makes opening difficult jars a breeze.

Quick Tip

MINI PIZZA BAGELS

2 bags mini bagels
1 (8 ounce) can pizza sauce
2 teaspoons oregano
Sliced mushrooms
Sliced pepperoni
Minced onions
Minced green bell peppers
Shredded mozzarella cheese

....

Preheat oven to 450 degrees. Split bagels in half and place on baking sheet, cut side up. Top each half with pizza sauce and other ingredients as desired, ending with cheese. Bake 10 to 12 minutes or until cheese melts and begins to bubble.

ARTICHOKE DIP

1 (10 ounce) package frozen artichoke hearts
1 cup sour cream
1 cup mayonnaise
½ cup grated Parmesan cheese

....

Preheat oven to 375 degrees. Thaw artichoke hearts and drain. In large bowl, combine sour cream, mayonnaise, and Parmesan cheese. Add artichoke hearts and mix thoroughly. Put mixture in baking dish and bake 35 minutes until hot and bubbly. Serve with crackers.

MEEMAW'S SWEET TEA

4 family-size tea bags
1½ cups sugar

....

Bring 1 quart water to boil. Add tea bags and let water continue to boil for 2 minutes, watching carefully. Cover with lid and let steep 8 minutes. Remove tea bags after squeezing remaining water out of bags. Immediately add sugar and stir until dissolved. Pour 1 quart lukewarm water into 2-quart pitcher. Then pour concentrated tea mixture into pitcher. Stir and pour over ice.

STRAWBERRY LEMONADE

1 tablespoon strawberry syrup
Juice from 1 lemon
2 teaspoons powdered sugar
Shaved ice
Water

....

Mix strawberry syrup, lemon juice, and powdered sugar in a glass. Add shaved ice. Add enough water to fill glass and stir well.

OLIVE SPREAD

1 (16 ounce) package cream cheese, softened
1 package ranch dressing mix
2 cans ripe olives
1 (11 ounce) can whole kernel corn
1 (4 ounce) can green chilies
1 medium red bell pepper
Tortilla chips

Beat cream cheese and dressing mix in large bowl until smooth. Drain olives and corn. Chop olives, green chilies, and bell pepper. Add all ingredients except tortilla chips to cheese mixture and mix well. Cover and refrigerate 1 to 2 hours until well chilled. Serve with tortilla chips.

DEVILED EGGS

6 hard-boiled eggs
¼ cup mayonnaise
1 teaspoon mustard
Salt and pepper to taste
Sweet paprika

Halve hard-boiled eggs lengthwise and remove yolks. Place yolks in bowl and mash with fork to desired consistency. Add mayonnaise and mustard. Mix well. Season with salt and pepper to taste. Stuff egg white halves with yolk mixture, dividing yolk mixture evenly among eggs. Sprinkle paprika lightly over eggs and refrigerate.

CUCUMBER FINGER SANDWICHES

4 ounces cream cheese, softened
½ cup mayonnaise
3 teaspoons grated cucumber
I teaspoon grated onion
2 drops green food coloring
Lemon juice to taste
Bread of choice

....

In bowl, cream all ingredients together except
lemon juice and bread. Add lemon juice to taste.
Serve between crustless bread or on crackers.

EASY MEATBALLS IN HAWAIIAN SAUCE

1 package frozen, fully cooked
  Italian-style meatballs
5 cups sweet-and-sour sauce

....

Combine meatballs and sauce in slow cooker.
Cook 2 hours on high. Serve with toothpicks. Also
great served over rice as a meal.

KITCHEN FLOSS

Keep some unflavored dental floss with your kitchen tools. It often works better than a knife to cleanly cut foods like soft cheese, rolled dough, layered cake, and cheesecake.

Quick Tip

DILL DIP

3 ounces cream cheese, softened
1 tablespoon finely chopped stuffed green olives
1 teaspoon grated onion
¼ teaspoon dried dill weed
Dash salt
1 tablespoon light cream

Put cream cheese in mixing bowl. Add green olives, grated onion, dill weed, and dash of salt, and mix well. Stir in light cream until mixture reaches dip consistency. Chill. Serve with veggies.

Cereal & Breads

Jesus replied, "I am the bread of life. Whoever comes to me will never be hungry again. Whoever believes in me will never be thirsty."
JOHN 6:35

8 cups whole oats
1½ cups bran
1½ cups wheat germ
1 cup coconut
¾ cup brown sugar
1 cup pecans
¾ cup canola oil
1 cup honey
2 teaspoons vanilla

Preheat oven to 325 degrees. In large bowl, mix oats, bran, wheat germ, coconut, brown sugar, and pecans. Heat canola oil, honey, and vanilla in small saucepan to boil. Pour over oat mixture. Mix well and spread in 2 greased 9x13-inch baking pans. Bake until golden brown, 25 to 30 minutes. Check and stir every 10 minutes. Remove from oven, pour onto trays, and cool 2 hours. Store in airtight container.

2 eggs
Pinch salt
2 cups sifted cornmeal
1 teaspoon baking soda
1 pint buttermilk

Preheat oven to 350 degrees. In bowl, beat eggs lightly. Add pinch of salt and cornmeal; mix. In separate bowl, dissolve baking soda in buttermilk and blend into cornmeal mixture. Pour into well-greased loaf pans and bake 35 minutes or until crust is a nice brown. Serve immediately.

ENGLISH MUFFINS

1 package dry yeast	1 teaspoon salt
1/4 cup warm water	4 cups sifted flour,
1 cup scalded milk	divided
3 tablespoons butter	1 egg
2 tablespoons sugar	Cornmeal

. . . .

Dissolve yeast in warm water. In large bowl, combine milk, butter, sugar, and salt. Cool milk mixture to lukewarm and stir in 2 cups flour. Add yeast mixture and egg, beating thoroughly. Add remaining flour or enough to make moderately soft dough. Turn out on lightly floured board and knead until smooth. Place dough in buttered bowl and cover with light towel. Let rise 1 hour in warm place until doubled in size. Punch down, then let rest for 10 minutes. Roll out 1/4-inch thick on board lightly covered with cornmeal. Cut into 3-inch rounds. Sprinkle tops with cornmeal, cover with dry towel and let rise on board about 45 minutes or until doubled in size. Cook slowly on ungreased heavy griddle. For each batch of muffins have griddle hot at first and reduce heat to brown them slowly. Cook each side 8 minutes.

HUSH PUPPIES

Oil
2 cups yellow cornmeal
2 tablespoons flour
1 tablespoon sugar
2 teaspoons salt
Pepper to taste
Hot water
¼ cup milk
¼ cup finely chopped onion
1 egg
2 teaspoons baking powder

Heat oil in deep skillet or fryer to 375 degrees.
Mix all dry ingredients except baking powder.
Pour in enough hot water to make thick mush,
making sure all ingredients are moist. Add milk,
onion, egg, and baking powder and mix thoroughly.
Use small ice-cream scoop to drop spoonfuls of
mixture into hot oil, and fry until golden brown.

2 cups sifted flour
Dash salt
2 teaspoons baking powder
1¾ cups milk
2 cups oil
Powdered sugar

In large bowl, mix together flour, salt, and baking powder. Add milk and stir. Roll out dough and cut into small triangles. Heat oil in deep fryer or deep skillet. Make sure fry bread is submerged in hot oil. Fry until golden brown, then top with sprinkle of powdered sugar and let cool.

BARN-RAISING BISCUITS

1 cup whole-wheat flour
2 cups all-purpose flour
2 tablespoons sugar
½ teaspoon salt
4½ teaspoons baking powder
¾ teaspoon cream of tartar
¾ cup butter or margarine
1 cup milk
1 egg

Preheat oven to 450 degrees. Combine flours,
sugar, salt, baking powder, and cream of tartar
in bowl. Cut in butter until mixture resembles
thick cornmeal. Quickly stir in milk and egg. Turn
out dough on floured cutting board and knead
lightly. Roll or pat out to 1-inch thickness. Cut
into 2-inch biscuits. Place on greased baking sheet.
Bake 12 to 15 minutes.

1 quart milk
½ cup butter
Grits
1 cup grated swiss cheese
Salt and pepper to taste
⅓ cup grated Parmesan cheese

Preheat oven to 375 degrees. In saucepan, bring milk and butter to slow boil and slowly add grits, stirring until mixture becomes thick. Transfer to bowl and beat grits with mixer for 5 minutes until creamy. Add swiss cheese and salt and pepper to taste. Pour into 2-quart greased casserole dish and sprinkle with Parmesan cheese. Bake 35 minutes.

The oven is a great place to have your dough do its rising. It's dark, out of the way, and you can make it warm and humid without turning on the oven. Place a shallow dish filled halfway with hot water below your rising dough to create the perfect environment for your dough to grow!

Quick Tip

DATE BREAD

1 cup chopped walnuts
½ teaspoon salt
1 cup pitted, chopped dates
1½ teaspoons baking soda
¼ cup shortening
¼ cup boiling water
2 eggs
1 teaspoon vanilla
1 cup sugar
1½ cups sifted flour

Preheat oven to 350 degrees. Grease 5x9-inch loaf pan and line with wax paper. With all ingredients at room temperature, combine nuts, salt, dates, and baking soda in bowl. Add shortening and water. Stir and set aside. In separate bowl, beat eggs until foamy. Add vanilla, sugar, and flour. Beat at medium speed. Add date mixture and beat well. Bake 1 hour and then let cool 10 minutes in pan before removing to serve.

BACON-ONION PAN ROLLS

1 pound frozen bread dough, thawed
¼ cup butter, melted and divided
½ pound sliced bacon, cooked and crumbled
½ cup chopped onion

On lightly floured board, roll dough to ¼-inch thickness. Cut into rounds using a 2½-inch biscuit cutter. Brush rounds using 3 tablespoons melted butter. Place 1 teaspoon each of bacon and onion on half of each round. Fold over and pinch to seal. With pinched sides up, place rolls in a greased 9-inch square baking pan, forming 3 rows of 6. Brush tops with remaining butter. Let rise until doubled in size, about 30 minutes. Bake at 350 degrees for 25 to 30 minutes or until golden brown.

BLUEBERRY BREAD

2 cups flour
1 cup sugar
1½ teaspoons baking powder
½ teaspoon baking soda
¼ teaspoon salt
2 tablespoons shortening
1 egg
Boiling water
¼ cup orange juice
1 tablespoon grated orange rind
1 cup blueberries
½ cup chopped walnuts

. . . .

Preheat oven to 350 degrees. Grease 5x9-inch loaf pan. In large bowl, mix flour, sugar, baking powder, baking soda, and salt thoroughly. Cut in shortening. Stir in egg. Add enough boiling water to orange juice and rind to measure 1 cup. Stir into flour mixture. Fold in blueberries and nuts. Pour batter into prepared pan. Bake 60 minutes.

1 pound flour
1 ounce yeast
Salt to taste
1 cup warm milk
1 ounce butter

Preheat oven to 350 degrees. Pour flour into bowl. Make a hole in center of flour, and pour in yeast and salt. Cover with cloth and leave in warm place for 3 hours. Knead to light dough with warm milk. Leave dough in warm place for 30 minutes. Then turn dough out onto lightly floured board and make into any fancy shapes. Let rise for a while. Brush rolls with a little milk or melted butter, and bake 15 to 20 minutes.

2 cups leftover cooked rice
1 cup milk
1 tablespoon margarine
¼ cup raisins or dates
Dash salt

Combine rice, milk, margarine, raisins or dates, and dash of salt in medium saucepan. Stir mixture over medium heat until margarine is melted. Simmer 1 to 2 minutes to thicken. Serve hot, with cream, sugar, and cinnamon added at the table to individual taste.

MONKEY BREAD

2½ cups sugar, divided
1 cup cinnamon
3 cans refrigerated biscuits
1 tablespoon vanilla
1 cup margarine

. . . .

Preheat oven to 350 degrees. In bowl, mix together 1 cup sugar and cinnamon. Quarter biscuits and roll them in sugar mixture. Place in 9x13-inch baking pan. Sprinkle remaining sugar mixture over biscuits. Set aside. Melt together vanilla, 1½ cups sugar, and margarine and pour over biscuits. Bake 30 minutes.

1 cup water
¼ cup apple juice
1 tart apple, diced
⅔ cup rolled oats
Dash cinnamon
1 cup skim milk

Place water, juice, and diced apple in medium saucepan and bring to boil. Stir in rolled oats and dash of cinnamon. Return to boil; reduce heat and simmer until thick. Serve hot with milk.

ZUCCHINI BREAD

2 cups grated zucchini
3 eggs
1 cup vegetable oil
2 cups sugar
3 teaspoons vanilla
3 cups flour
1 teaspoon salt
1 teaspoon cinnamon
¼ teaspoon baking powder
1 teaspoon baking soda
½ cup nuts

. . . .

Preheat oven to 350 degrees. In large bowl, mix all ingredients well. Bake in 2 greased loaf pans for 1 hour. Tip: Use waxed paper across the bottom of the greased pans for easy removal.

To keep homemade bread crust crisp, store the bread in a brown paper bag or let it just sit on the countertop. Storing bread in plastic wrap or in a plastic bag will soften the crust quickly.

Quick Tip

JOHNNY CAKE CORN BREAD

¾ cup flour
1 teaspoon baking soda
2 tablespoons sugar
½ teaspoon salt
1¼ cups cornmeal
2 eggs
¼ cup vinegar
¼ cup melted butter

. . . .

Preheat oven to 400 degrees. Into bowl, sift together flour, baking soda, sugar, and salt and then stir in cornmeal. In separate bowl, whisk together eggs, vinegar, and butter. Add to dry ingredients and mix until moist. Grease 9-inch baking dish. Pour in batter and bake for 30 minutes to a light brown.

PUMPKIN BREAD

3 ½ cups flour
2 ½ cups sugar
1 ½ teaspoons salt
2 teaspoons baking soda
1 ½ teaspoons cinnamon
1 teaspoon nutmeg
1 (16 ounce) can pumpkin purée
1 cup vegetable oil
4 eggs

Preheat oven to 350 degrees. Grease and flour two loaf pans. In large bowl, mix flour, sugar, salt, baking soda, cinnamon, and nutmeg. In separate bowl, stir together pumpkin and oil. Beat eggs into dry mixture, one at a time, beating well after each addition. Add pumpkin mixture. Stir until dry ingredients are moist. Pour batter into prepared pans. Bake 1 hour.

BROWN SODA BREAD

1¾ cups all-purpose flour
1 teaspoon salt
1 teaspoon baking soda
2¼ cups whole-wheat flour
2 tablespoons margarine
1¼ cups buttermilk

Preheat oven to 375 degrees. Sift all-purpose flour, salt, and baking soda into bowl. Stir in whole-wheat flour. Cut in margarine. Add buttermilk and knead until smooth. Place on greased baking sheet. Bake 40 minutes. Allow to cool before cutting.

HONEY PEANUT BUTTER CEREAL BARS

1 cup peanut butter
⅔ cup honey
4 cups crispy rice cereal
2 cups fruit/nut cereal of choice

In saucepan over medium heat, melt peanut butter and honey until creamy. Add in cereals until well mixed. Spread onto wax paper and let cool before cutting into bars.

SPIFFY BISCUITS

1 package dry yeast
¾ cup warm water
½ teaspoon salt
3 tablespoons sugar
2 tablespoons oil
2 cups flour

. . . .

Preheat oven to 400 degrees. In large bowl, mix
yeast with warm water. Stir in salt, sugar, and
oil. Add flour. Roll out dough on lightly floured
surface and cut out biscuit rounds. Place in
greased pan. Let rise 30 minutes. Bake until golden
brown, approximately 8 to 10 minutes.

GLAZED LEMON BREAD

¾ cup margarine
1½ cups sugar
3 eggs
2¼ cups flour
¼ teaspoon salt
¼ teaspoon baking soda
¾ cup buttermilk
Zest from 2 lemons

Glaze:
¾ cup sugar
Juice from 2 lemons

In large bowl, cream together margarine and sugar. Beat in eggs. In separate bowl, mix flour, salt, and baking soda. Starting with dry mixture, add dry mixture and buttermilk alternately to margarine mixture, stirring after each addition. Stir in lemon zest. Pour into greased loaf pan. Bake at 350 degrees for 1 hour. Glaze: In small bowl, mix sugar and lemon juice until sugar dissolves. When bread is done but still warm, pierce bread with fork and drizzle glaze over top.

KONA BREAD

½ cup butter or margarine
1 cup sugar
2 eggs
¾ cup very ripe bananas
1¼ cups sifted all-purpose flour
¾ teaspoon baking soda
½ teaspoon salt

Preheat oven to 350 degrees. In large bowl, cream butter and sugar until fluffy. Add eggs, one at a time, beating well after each. Mash bananas and stir in. Sift dry ingredients together into banana mixture and mix well. Pour into well-greased loaf pan. Bake 35 minutes.

MAPLE ALMOND GRANOLA

3 cups maple syrup
1 teaspoon almond extract
2 teaspoons orange zest
2 cups rolled oats
2 cups puffed-rice cereal
2 cups puffed-wheat cereal
⅓ cup wheat germ
2 cups puffed corn cereal
1 teaspoon cinnamon

Preheat oven to 350 degrees. Boil liquids in large pot until mixture foams and rises, only a few minutes. Quickly stir in remaining ingredients. Spread mixture onto 9x13-inch baking dish. Bake 10 to 15 minutes until golden and crunchy. Watch closely the last few minutes because it can burn quickly. Remove from oven and press lightly with spatula. Let cool, then break apart to serve.

The easiest way to test if your bread is done is to insert a butter knife into the center. If it comes out clean, your baking is complete.

Quick Tip

143

BUTTERMILK WHEAT BREAD

2 cups white whole-wheat flour
1 cup all-purpose flour
½ teaspoon salt
1 teaspoon baking soda
2 tablespoons sugar
2 tablespoons butter
1 egg
1⅓ cups buttermilk
½ cup chopped pecans

Preheat oven to 350 degrees. In large bowl, combine dry ingredients. Stir in remaining ingredients and mix well. Place in greased loaf pan and bake 35 minutes.